God's Love:
Nothing Compares

BETTY M. CROSS

Anchor Strong Books
Houston

Copyright © 2019 by B. Cross Publishing LLC.

All rights reserved. No portion of this book may be reproduced, stored in a retrieval system, or transmitted in any form by any means—electronic, mechanical, photocopy, recording, scanning, or other—except for brief quotations in critical reviews or articles, without the prior written permission of the publisher.

Scripture taken from the New King James Version. Copyright © 1982 by Thomas Nelson, Inc. Used by permission. All rights reserved.

For information contact:
staff@bcrosspublishing.com
www.bcrosspublishing.com

Library of Congress Cataloging-in-Publication Data

Cross, Betty M.
    God's Love: Nothing Compares/ Betty M. Cross
    p. cm.
    ISBN 978-1-7339295-0-9

Printed in the United States of America

God's Love:
Nothing Compares

Dedicated to my loving parents,
Holton Stallworth Sr. (1925-1994)
and Paralee Stallworth (1928-1993);
My examples of God's love,
who poured into me and countless others
from the abundance of His love

Contents

Acknowledgements: xi
Introduction: Deeper Call to Love: xiii

PART 1: WHO CAN DEFINE LOVE?

Chapter 1: What is Love?   21
        Greek Love
        God is the Source
        Apart From God's Love
        Questions and Misconceptions

Chapter 2: Greater Than Love   33
        God Loves Us
        God Always Had Us in Mind
        God Knows All About Us
        Everlasting Love
        Beyond Love

PART 2: HIS LOVE CHANGES US

Chapter 3: Our Identity in Jesus   45
        A New Creation
        New Garments
        We Are Accepted and Secure
        We Are Heirs of God
        We Are Unique and Have Great Value
        We Have Purpose
        Confidence in the Lord

Chapter 4: Self-Love   59
    Learn to Accept Yourself
    Continuous Growth and Development
    Components of Wholeness
    Physical Wellness
    Emotional and Mental Wellness
    Intellectual Wellness
    Social Wellness
    Environmental Wellness
    Occupational Wellness
    Financial Wellness
    Spiritual Wellness

Chapter 5: Abide in Me   75
    Trusting God
    What Can Separate Us?

PART 3: LOVING AND SERVING OTHER

Chapter 6: Unity   83
    Covenant Relationships
    Loving Others as Ourselves
    Marriage
    Singleness
    Unity Theme

Chapter 7: Challenging Relationships   99
    Bad Company
    Misunderstandings
    Gossip
    Insecurities
    Pride
    Jealousy
    Hatred

Chapter 8: Forgiveness   113
    When Conflict Arises
    Handling Offense
    Reconciliation

Appendix   123
Endnotes   127
About the Author   129

Acknowledgments

I am forever thankful for all the wonderful people God placed in my life over the years that contributed to this project. I pray God will add blessings on top of blessings to all those who prayed; inspired, encouraged, and loved me thru it all. There are too many to name—but you all know who you are—I thank, and love you with the love of the Lord.

To my family—May these words be embraced from generation to generation. I love you all.

To my beloved friend-sister, Kori Harakel—who believed in me and prayed for me when I wanted to quit. I love and miss you dearly.

Above all, to My Lord and Savior Jesus Christ—giving glory and honor to the One faithful God, without Him, none of this would have been possible.

Introduction

Deeper Call to Love

THE LOVE OF GOD is limitless and we can never receive too much. Since the dimensions of God's love—length, breadth, depth, and height never cease, our passionate pursuit to receive more should not either. God continually calls us to greater measures of His abundant love and our obedience pleases Him. Regardless of the timespan in relationship with God, days or decades, He earnestly wants to deposit more of His Spirit (love) into our lives. Beyond all we think there is to know about God's love, we can always experience more and tap into deeper intimacy.

Seeking God's love is a deliberate act and when we set aside time and position our heart to commune with Him, more is revealed about His love. Actively pursuing the love of God transforms and strengthens our lives. In His presence, we receive nourishment in every area of our life because we are connecting to the source of life and love.

A progressive relationship with God also restores and heals us; allowing us to truly love ourselves and others. Once we personally accept God's love, others also benefit in meaningful ways, because now we can give them genuine love.

Introduction

Engaging in ongoing fellowship with our Maker opens the door for us to receive fresh revelation from God to victoriously carryout our purpose on earth.

Anything we do without the love of God working thru us; including operating in our gifts and talents, are meaningless and lacks effectiveness in the eyes of God. Our actions then are carnal; dissatisfying, and does not display the true nature of God functioning thru us. In other words, we are likened to an annoying instrument needing to be fine-tuned. In this manner, we make noise but sound repulsive and our intended purpose is not realized. We are like a song without key elements; merely reduced to a poem. In contrast, abiding in the love of God pleases Him and empowers us to carry out our purpose on earth with passion and victory. God is love and to receive the fullness of His love, we must surrender our life to Him. Connecting to His love requires our willingness.

Trusting Him whole-heartedly demonstrates our total reliance, acceptance and confidence in Him alone. Though He has wonderful plans for our life, our free will can either except or reject God's plan for our life. Our heavenly Father is gentle and loving therefore, we must give Him permission to take residency in all chambers of our heart and surrender our life to Him.

New dimensions of intimacy and closeness are granted when we give God full access to all areas of our life without restriction and limitation. Honest and open communion with God clears the pathway to a deeper relationship with God. In this manner, entrance is given to the innermost parts of our soul and our relationship with God becomes more intimate.

For so long, I thought I knew what love was all about, but God's love had not yet infiltrated my heart because of my resistance, which created was blockage. My idea of love came from a limited perception, yet I knew something was missing. As I surrendered my life to God everything changed for my good.

Allowing Jesus to heal the painful areas of my heart has been no easy process and continues as He continues to strip away layers that have accumulated over the years. However, the journey has all been worth fully surrendering my heart and life to God and allowing Him to heal my soul from a traumatic past.

My biological mother, whom I have never met, was raped and consequently my twin brother and I were conceived. At two weeks old, we were adopted and raised by a loving, God-fearing, middle-class family. Although they had seven older children, they chose to adopt my twin and I, and also cared for numerous foster children; often in crisis situations. They loved us as their own and did so with the love of God. Tragically, at age thirteen I watched my mother take her last breath after suffering an ugly battle with leukemia. Six months later, my dad passed away also from stomach cancer and possibly a broken heart because he loved "Honey," whom he had been married to nearly four decades.

After their passing, a lot changed because life as I knew it changed. No longer did I feel secure or loved, but numb and traumatized. Something died inside. I was also separated from my foster brothers and sisters who went to different homes

Introduction

while my twin and I moved from California to New Jersey with my older brother and his family. We lived there for a year before returning to California to live with another older brother and his family. A year later, we moved again and with each move, the heavy burden of two teenagers being placed on others was felt. The once stable middle-class childhood I knew was flipped upside down. As my surroundings changed, my quality of living did as well and before long, I was living in dangerous neighborhoods, and connected to street life. Surprisingly, I was able to keep exceptional grades and leadership roles from middle thru high school. While going to school, I worked full-time, ran track, and cross-country. At sixteen, my twin and I were separated and by seventeen, I was on my own.

    I always knew God was with me and "loved me," but soon forgot because of everything happening in my life at the time. After losing my parents, I became heartbroken and overwhelmed with feelings of hopelessness and sadness. It seemed as no one cared or could relate to what I was experiencing, which made me become indrawn. One day I sat on the bathroom floor with scissors in my hand and just as the thought entered my mind to end all the pain for good, I remembered my twin brother and that God loved me and had a purpose for my life. I thought, maybe if I could hold on one more day tomorrow would be better.

    Over many years of feeling unwanted and unloved I began searching for answers and love in all the wrong places. I experienced extreme rejection; abandonment, heartbreak, violence, and betrayal during my adolescence. Each day I woke up believing God had a plan for my life because of all I endured. Although I did not always know my worth, I knew God loved me and if I held on, things would get better. However, things got worse before getting better and a pattern of entering into toxic relationships developed, and my first marriage was no exception. After divorcing, I quickly remarried only to realize it was to fill a void. Right away, I knew I made a big mistake and divorced soon after. As I got closer to God and allowed Him to heal the painful areas in my life, He began to heal my soul and uncover more areas that were not yet healed. The love of God changed my life.

Nothing compares to the love of God and seeking His love is vital to an abundant life. Surrendering my heart to God brought confidence in learning He loves and accepts me as I am, and my pursuit of His love began from that revelation. As we dig into the love of God—rooted and grounded; my hope is that all those wanting to experience more of God's love, as well as those searching for "true love," will be overwhelmed by the goodness of His love, mercy, and grace. May His perfect love be revealed like never before as we greatly expect to answer the call of richly embracing His love!

Betty M. Cross

PART: 1

Who Can Define Love

Chapter 1

What is Love?

BY NO MEANS is this an attempt to define God's love. Neither is this a revelation of all there is to know thereof, because that is impossible. Instead, the intent here is geared towards living a lifestyle which embodies the ongoing exploration of the love of God. Jesus constantly calls us to experience more of His love, consequently it is more than a one-time encounter and new dimensions are discovered in seeking out His limitless love.

To set the framework that differentiates God's true love from others, we briefly glance at various "types of *love*," definitions, usages and misconceptions. Additionally, we look at how living separated from God disconnects us from the Source of love. Again, the focus here is not on defining God's love but rather to give a backdrop of the variations before intimately searching out the richness of God's love.

An interest in love is sought amongst humanity regardless of age; gender, race, religion or economic background. To some degree, people desire love whether they admit or not and the desire for love is seen in many aspects of life. Love remains a hot topic for discussion because it is powerful; capable of changing people, crosses cultures, unites the worst of enemies, ends wars, and creates unity and peace. Countless movies are centered on the subject of love. Love is discussed thoroughly; written of extensively, and passionately sung about throughout the world. It is believed by some that love is an action displayed or an emotion felt; yet others believe both. Love can be a noun (person, place, or thing) or a verb (an action; occurrence or state of being).

Webster's dictionary defines love both in noun and verb forms. As a noun love is: an intense feeling of deep affection; a great interest and pleasure in something; a person or thing that one loves; nil (a score of zero; in tennis, squash, and some other sports); and as a verb love is: to feel a deep romantic or sexual attachment to (someone).[1]

Another version of love according to Vines's dictionary offers the following definition in verb form: *'ahab' or 'aheb,'* the Hebrew word meaning to love; like i.e., a strong emotional attachment to and desire either to possess or to be in the presence of the object; familial, romantic or friendship. The noun form of love: *'ahabah;'* is the Hebrew word meaning love; and haves the same meaning as the verb form; refers also to sexual love as a state of being or strong affection and commitment.

The topic of love is a big deal; however, the word *love* sometimes is used with little thought and regard to its meaning. Vast explanations are adopted to describe and express love, but the true definition of love is 1 Corinthians 13:4-8:

> *Love suffers long and is kind; love does not envy; love does not parade itself, it is not puffed up; does not behave rudely, does not seek its own, is not provoked, thinks no evil; does not rejoice in iniquity, but rejoices in the truth; bears all things, believes all things, hopes all things, endures all things. Love never fails....*

Greek Love

The ancient Greeks categorized love into many facets. To gain a broader understanding, each is summarized as follow:

Agape is selfless; charity; unconditional; and spiritual love; a love for everyone. It accepts and forgives (repeatedly); believes for the greater good; loves free from expectations, regardless of the flaws or shortcomings of others. In Greek culture, it is the highest and most radical type of love. Note: agape is often used to describe God's love because it closely resembles it, but God's love is much more than agape or unconditional and cannot be fully described. Keep this in mind where agape is used to reference the love of God.

Eros, which is named after the Greek god of love and fertility is sensual, romantic love centered on selfishness; physical pleasure, and infatuation. It also is the root of "erotic" and the physical body usually causes this love to manifest. When misused or indulged it often leads to impulsive acts and broken hearts.

Ludus is a playful; flirty, euphoric love. Frequently seen between young lovers in the early stages of falling in love. Emotions cause this type of love to surface.

Mania love is obsessive; crazy, possessive love due to desiring a sense of value. Commonly seen by those with low self-esteem, who become jealous; dependent or have feelings of desperately "needing" another. Mania is seen in relationships where love is solely based as the means of survival.

Pragma is mature love; enduring, longstanding, aged, and rational love developing over time. Often displayed between married couples or friendships formed over time. This love is seen among those who learn to compromise; and demonstrate patience and tolerance.

Storge is a natural; familiar love without physical attraction. Storge is commonly seen between parents and children or childhood friends that continue into adulthood. Usually this love develops by causal memories and familiarity.

Philia is brotherly; affectionate love; likened to deep friendship. In Greek culture, it is considered love between equals, and closely resembles phileo, the Hebrew word meaning "lover of" and the derivative of the following combinations: philotheos, meaning "a lover of God," philoxenos, meaning "loving strangers;" philagathos, meaning "loving that which is good;" philarguros, "loving money;" philedonos, "loving pleasure;" philautos, "selfishly loving oneself" in a negative manner and is displayed in 2 Timothy 3:2.[3]

Philautia is self-love in a healthy fashion. Philautia differs from *philautos*, an egotistic; narcissistic, conceited approach taken in seeking one's own interest. Self-love (philautia) is understanding that to genuinely love others, we must first receive God's love and love ourselves in order to give love to others. Philautia is not vain self-obsession, nor does it focus on obtaining fame or gaining fortune. In Greek culture, the common belief is to care for others, one must first learn to care for his or her self.

Self-love (philautia) is discussed in greater detail in chapter four, because to love others genuinely, we must first love ourselves. How can we give love to another if we do not first love the person God created? Under these circumstances, we will not be able to genuinely love others, since lacking self-love makes it impossible to love authentically.

First, God's love must be received before developing philautia (self-love), then we are able to love and serve others meaningfully. Although we have covered many forms of love, as we continue to seek the love of God, our understanding broadens as we gain an even better perspective of the love of God.

God is the Source

God literally is love! Therefore, no one can love us better than God. Receiving and knowing God is receiving and knowing His true love. God is the source of love.

In 1 John 4:16 we see the perfect illustration:

> *And we have known and believed the love that God has for us. God is love, and he who abides in love abides in God, and God in him.*

God is the source of love and when we connect to God, we connect directly to love. Fully abiding in God brings healing and wholeness that transforms our life. As we draw close to Jesus; abiding and resting, He fills us with Himself—love. Take a moment to process the fact that God is love and love is God. Selah (pause) and take this truth to heart.

Apart From God's Love

Living apart from God, the source of love, causes hopelessness and emptiness inside. We were not designed to live apart from God. We detect that there is something missing when He is not involved in our life. A longing deep within is felt by not accepting God's love. Even if at some point we received Him but stopped seeking Him regularly, we sense a void because contentment is found in Jesus alone.

Nothing in this world can substitute for the love of God or provide the care we need as God does. Seeking love outside of God is an empty pursuit that causes one to desperately try to fill the void with something. Looking for love and contentment in anything besides Jesus leads to destruction and frustration because only God completes us, and anything else will fall short. Being unaware of this truth will cause people to dangerously seek love in all the wrong places, since the Love of God cannot be replaced. Anything attempting to do so is a counterfeit or replica that will be short-lived and provide temporal satisfaction. At some point, we all have tried to fill areas of our life with empty pursuits. Some common things that tug at the hearts of many people and give false gratification include; money, relationships, gambling, drugs, alcohol, food, shopping, sex, working out and career advancement. The list could continue because it is anything that we have placed before God.

An individual may find temporary relief in these things but remains frustrated and void until he or she decides to receive God's love. Psalm 34:18 tells us, *"The Lord is near to those who have a broken heart, and saves such as have a contrite spirit."* Only God can fix the brokenness in our lives and the key is realizing He alone fills our emptiness. Only in Jesus do we find wholeness.

Questions and Misconceptions

To expose some distortions and tactics used to keep people in bondage we glance at a few lies of the enemy. Many ask: Does God love me? Can we really love unconditionally? Yes, and yes! God loves us like none other and never ceases despite our shortcomings. His love is unconditional and beyond comprehension. Once we receive the love of God we can choose to give it to others. Other areas about God's love that need clarification include the following misconceptions:

Misconception: A marriage makes one more valuable and loved.

False. Marriage does not make us whole or more valuable. Many couples marry believing things somehow get better once they become one. Consequently, they suffer behind closed doors thinking their problems vanish after marriage. Understand, marriage does not lift problems or unresolved personal issues one has prior to the union and after marriage, one must continue abiding in God's love as their source.

Misconception: Doing good deeds save me.

False. Anyone is capable of doing a good deed, including those who have never accepted Jesus into their heart. Doing kind acts do not save us, accepting Jesus as our Savior does. (To accept Jesus into your heart now, see appendix).

Misconception: True love can be found in relationships outside of a personal relationship with God.

False. Relationships with others are important however, no relationship, including marriage compares to our relationship with God.

Misconception: God loves some people more than others.

False. Unfortunately, many believe God loves them more because they are special or served Him for many years, however this is far from true. God loves us all without partiality. Further, the time one has known God does not determine the level of intimacy one has with Him because that comes thru spending time with God. For instance, a child who accepted Jesus but never spent time getting to know Him over the years, remains a babe in Christ. Another who recently accepted Him, but spends regular time getting to know Him, may be more spiritually mature than the previous. Spirit maturity is not based on age or when one accepted God, because that only comes from regular fellowship with Him. God loves us all uniquely the same. *"For there is no partiality with God"* (Romans 2:11), and is further explained in Romans 10:12, *"For there is no distinction between Jew and Greek, for the same Lord over all is rich to all who call upon Him."* God loves us all and no one is more important than another person.

Misconception: Doing good deeds shows God's love operating in me.

False. Anyone is capable of doing a good deed, including those who never accepted Jesus into their heart. Doing nice things does not mean we operate in the love of God nor are we saved by our good deeds.

Misconception: God is angry and distant.

False. Going thru hard times may cause us to conclude that God is mad with us. Many believe God stops loving them because of sin or disobedience, while He hates all sin, He loves us even when we sin. Deuteronomy 31:8 says, *"And the LORD, He is the One who goes before you. He will be with you, He will not leave you nor forsake you; do not fear nor be dismayed"* He is with us always and never distant.

Misconception: God does not love me.

False. God loves us and desires that none perish. Not only does He love us now, but while knowing all we would do, good and bad, before we were even born, and His love never stops.

Misconception: Love involves pain or abuse.

False. Unfortunately, many think they are loved by the complexity of their relationship, because love requires pain and abuse. However, the opposite is true, because those who truly love us do not inflict physically or verbally abuse on us.

Greater Than Love

Chapter 2

Greater Than Love

THROUGHOUT THE BIBLE God gave us specific instructions about love and He places great emphasis on it, therefore we should as well. Jesus tells us to love Him with all our heart, soul, mind and to love others as ourselves, (Matthew 22:37-39). God wants us to live abundantly, and tells us to abide in His love and keep all His Commandments. We are given specific instruction and promises by Jesus about His love. In John 15:9-10 Jesus says:

> *As the Father loved Me, I also have loved you; abide in My love. If you keep My commandments, you will abide in My love, just as I have kept My Father's commandments and abide in His love.*

We are to abide in His love. What does "abiding in His love" resemble? The word *abide* means, to wait for: await; to endure without yielding: withstand; to bear patiently; tolerate; to accept without objection; to remain stable or fixed in a state; to continue in a place; sojourn.[4] In Hebrew, the word *abide* has several meanings: *epimeno*, meaning: to abide in; continue in; tarry and indicates perseverance. *Katameno*, meaning: constant residence; frequent resort; and to wait. *Parameno*, meaning: to remain beside; and to continue near. *Hupomeno*, meaning: to abide under; to remain in a place instead of leaving it; and to stay behind. *Prosmeno*, meaning: to abide still longer; continue with; of cleaving unto a person; indicating persistent loyalty; and of continuing in a thing.[5] We are to remain in God's love and never be moved from that position.

Abiding in the love of God is an ongoing process and is covered in chapter five. Jesus says His love is perfected in us when we obey His Word (1 John 2:5-6). If we love God, we abide in His love and obey all His commandments and not just the ones that make us comfortable or those we deem valuable. God will correct us when we get off track because He loves us.

God Loves Us

God's love is expressed different from the ways of the world. Jesus wants us to search out the dimensions of His love for us. Typical worldly-love focuses on expressing ones feelings and finding ways to show love. According to Gary Chapman, author of *The Five Love Languages: How to Express Heartfelt Commitment to Your Mate*, five chief ways some express love include; buying gifts, spending quality time together, using words of affirmation, performing acts of service, and physical touch. All of these are positive ways to show love, however the love of God shown towards us exceeds them all and is far greater than what anyone could ever give us. That is why it is important for us to fill our voids with God's love.

Jesus expressed the highest form of love towards us by laying down His life for us while we were sinners. 1 John 4:9 says, *"in this the love of God was manifested toward us, that God has sent His only begotten Son into the world, that we might live through Him."* Few are willing to give up an only child; let alone make them a sacrifice.

Parents are extremely protective of their children and guard them at all cost. Similarly, God protects and wants us to live an abundant life. He made us alive in Jesus and seated us in heavenly places far above all things. John 3:16 tells us, *"For God so loved the world that He gave His only begotten Son, that whoever believes in Him should not perish but have everlasting life."* Additionally, Romans 5:8 pertains to God's love for us and states, *"But God demonstrates His own love toward us, in that while we were still sinners, Christ died for us."* God loves us so much that He gave His one and only Son that we might have life. Further, He wants us to live abundantly in Him! What great love He has for us!

Jesus demonstrated His love for us thru the ultimate sacrifice of laying down His life, although it was within His power to do otherwise. He loves us so much that He did this while we were sinners. Since He paid the price for all our sins, we can come to Him and confess our sin when we fall short. We do not have to pretend to have it all together because no one is perfect. Nothing we do catches Him off guard or causes

Him to love us less. We can rest well knowing Jesus knows and cares about every detail of our life. Although it may appear He does not see what we are currently experiencing, He knows everything about us and gave us everything we need to live victoriously! In Matthew 6:31-34, Jesus says:

> *Therefore do not worry, saying, 'What shall we eat?' or 'What shall we drink?' or 'What shall we wear?' For after all these things the Gentiles seek. For your heavenly Father knows that you need all these things. But seek first the kingdom of God and His righteousness, and all these things shall be added to you.*

God knows our individual needs before we ever ask. By putting Him first in all areas of our life, we invite Him into our situation and do not need to worry about our needs being met.

As God's chosen people, He desires to give us an abundantly life, because He loves us so much. So that He could relate to us, He came to a sin-filled world to pull us out of darkness. He walked the earth and felt the emotions we feel today. "For we do not have a High Priest who cannot sympathize with our weaknesses, but was in all points tempted as we are, yet without sin" (Hebrews 4:15). He really knows how we feel and does not want us to live beneath what was provided for on the cross. Jesus knows all about everything we go thru in life and wants to help us live victoriously.

God Always Had Us in Mind

God's plans for us were established before the foundations of the world. Jeremiah 29:11 tells us, *"For I know the thoughts that I think toward you, says the LORD, thoughts of peace and not of evil, to give you a future and a hope."* Anything opposite of God's goodness comes from the enemy, whose job is to steal; kill and to destroy.

In Jesus, the victory is already ours! Psalm 139:17-18 says, *"How precious also are Your thoughts to me, O God! How great is the sum of them! If I should count them, they would be more in number than the sand..."* From the beginning, Jesus' plan and purpose for us has always been positive although it may not always seem that way. Jesus knew all about us before we were born, (see Romans 8:29-30).

God's thoughts of us are pleasant and bountiful. He delights in the prosperity of His people and not just from a financially standpoint. He takes pleasure in us and even sings over us. Imagine our heavenly Father smiling upon us and singing a lullaby to gently put us to rest, while knowing everything He knows about us. If God has good thoughts about us, then we should too. Remember, His thoughts about us are always good.

God Knows All About Us

Did you know that God knows more about us then we know about ourselves? After all, He did create us in His image and is in-tune with every intricate detail about our life. Jeremiah 1:5 tells us, *"Before I formed you in the womb I knew you; before you were born I sanctified you..."* To give an idea of just how acquainted He is with us, He knows the number of hairs we have on our head. God is familiar with every minute detail and body part; including our cells, because we were uniquely fashioned by God, (see Psalm 119:73). Considering all of humanity, it amazes me that no two people are the same. Since we all are different, there is something extremely special and unique each of us has to offer.

God made no mistake in creating us and loves us just as we are. Realizing that God made us should help us embrace who we are. Next time we start complaining about our flaws or body parts, remember each part was designed by the hand of God. It is insulting to criticize or belittle God's creation. The Master Architect created us from His divine blueprint. Certainly His creation is flawless because He makes no mistakes. Psalm 139:14-16 says:

> *I will praise You, for I am fearfully and wonderfully made; marvelous are Your works, and that my soul knows very well. My frame was not hidden from You, when I was made in secret, and skillfully wrought in the lowest parts of the earth. Your eyes saw my substance, being yet unformed. And in Your book they all were written, the days fashioned for me, when as yet there were none of them.*

As clay on a throw, each person is justifiably formed by The Potter who continues shaping us for His intended purposes.

The work He started in us He promised to complete. Nothing goes undetected by God, nor is there anything too great or small for Him concerning us. Absolutely nothing about us is unimportant to God, (see Psalm 139:1-3). He loves us with an everlasting love and wants to be involved in every aspect of our life.

Everlasting Love

God's love for us is everlasting—eternal, never-ending, perpetual, and endless; meaning it never stops, even when we are unfaithful towards Him. The love of God continues faithfully. Jeremiah 31:3 states, *"The Lord has appeared of old to me, saying: Yes, I have loved you with an everlasting love; therefore with lovingkindness I have drawn you."* The word *loving-kindness*; or *chesed* in Hebrew, closely defines God's love towards us. This love extends past unconditional and provides steadfast love; grace, mercy, faithfulness, and goodness.[6] God's love for us goes beyond agape and because it is unending, we should continue seeking and receiving the love of God relentlessly.

The love of God cannot be fully comprehended; however, we should have a newfound understanding for the wonderful phrase, "Jesus loves us." Understand, it is impossible for us to fully comprehend just how much He truly loves us, because not only is His love everlasting, it is beyond measure. As we continue seeking out the love of God, He reveals areas of our life we have not completely surrendered or given to Him; perhaps He already has. Take a moment to think about the everlasting love of God and the areas that need to be surrendered so He can enter. Life is much better trusting and surrendering to the One who knows all about us and loves us far beyond our understanding of love.

Beyond Love

God not only extends His love to us, but also mercy. The Greek word for mercy is *eleos* or *eleemon* (there are several others), meaning: sympathy and pity displayed by God for us. *Mercy* is seen thru God's care for us, because though it is within His power to punish us, instead He extends grace and compassion. The character of Christ, as the High Priest, is merciful towards us and not simply possessed of pity, but actively compassionate.[7] By mercy, we get an extension of God's love, which endures forever, (see Jude 1:21, Ephesians 2:4-5 and Psalm 136). God not only extends love and mercy, but also grace. In short, *grace* or *charis* in Greek is that which bestows or occasions pleasure; delight, or causes favorable regard; e.g., to beauty, or gracefulness of person and speech.[8] Grace is defined by many as God's unmerited favor or favorable regard towards us; and is seen in unlikely circumstances. In our weakness, grace yields remarkable results that undeniably come from God. By faith we receive grace and nothing we ever do makes us deserving, because if grace could be earned, then we would be able to boast about our works. Grace supplies much: by it, we are saved, strengthened, have access and peace with God thru Jesus, (see Ephesians 2:4-8; 2 Corinthians 12:9, and Romans 5:1-2).

Although God gives us grace, it does not mean we should live or act any kind of way we want. In other words, grace is not an excuse to live any way we desire because we know God will forgive us. There are consequences for abusing grace. Although no one is perfect, we should not practice sin.

IN THE NEXT SECTION, WE SEE HOW GOD'S LOVE CHANGES US.

Greater Than Love

PART 2:

His Love Changes Us

Our Identity in Jesus

Chapter 3

Our Identity in Jesus

KNOWLEDGE OF WHO we are in Jesus is extremely powerful because it allows us to clearly see ourselves as God sees us. Having the wrong view of who we are hinders us from moving forward in the plan God has for our life. Similarly, we do not have to agree with the opinions of others that fail to line up with our firm identity in Jesus Christ because He already affirmed us. Layer upon layer, we will look at our identity in Christ.

First, we must recognize we are already everything He says about us and receive it by faith. An understanding of our identity in Jesus teaches us how to carry ourselves in thought, speech and action. Most importantly, it prepares us for our destiny, because as we get closer to our Maker, we learn exactly who we are in Him. It also redirects us purposefully, because as we believe the truth, our thoughts change, and our speech synchronize with our thoughts. This is empowering because, the power of life and death is in the tongue (our speech), (see Proverbs 18:21).

The Bible tells us, what we think about ourselves, ultimately we become. *"For as he thinks in his heart, so is he"* (Proverbs 23:7). Therefore, we speak either life or death to our purpose accordingly.

Our actions also are governed by our thoughts. We do things according to what we believe. Do we know who we are in Jesus Christ? Considering all at stake, we should get an understanding, since our thoughts, speech, and actions are governed by who we believe we are in Jesus. Let us journey on and discover our true identity in Him.

It is important to know we are children of God and He loves us. 1 John 3:1 says, *"Behold what manner of love the Father has bestowed on us, that we should be called children of God!..."* Bestowed in context means, He presented that position to us as a gift. In Romans 8:14, our identity as children is reiterated and explains, *"For as many as are led by the Spirit of God, these are sons of God."* Now, we are children of God and not only are we children of God, but we are much more. For instance, though we are servants of God, we are also His friends and much more, (see John 15:13-15). A friend is someone we share a special bond with.

The Lord shows us our true identity—who we really are—thru His Word. By the Word, false labels; descriptors, and any other negative influences, get striped away. Our Maker knows us precisely and helps us put on our true identity.

A New Creation

Accepting Jesus into our heart as Lord and Savior makes us a new creation. No longer are we the same therefore we should live for the One who died and rose just for us. 1 Corinthians 5:17 tells us, *"Therefore, if anyone is in Christ, he is a new creation; old things have passed away; behold, all things have become new."* Now, the Holy Spirit lives inside of us.

Holding on to our old mindset is easy however, it must go in order to receive the fullness of what God has for our life. Rehearsing our past only causes us to lose focus and live stagnated lives. It also derails us from the path of our destiny, further preventing us from fully accessing all God has for us.

When we hold on to our past, it limits our thoughts about our new identity. What thoughts from the past are we maintaining? Maybe it was something that happened during childhood or later in life. How are these thoughts keeping us from moving forward? Are these thoughts based on things we used to do? Any thoughts from our past that do not align with our identity in Jesus are an attack from the enemy. To move forward, we can glance at our past but must choose not to stay there. We may even need to write down certain events to evaluate the impact it had on us or to figure out the steps to move forward. However, our past is our past. What we did just five-seconds ago is our past and we can decide to let the past go. Whether we choose to let our past go or to define us; the choice is completely ours. Easier said than done, right? Take a deep breath and release all negative and hindering thoughts of the past. Since we have decided to let the past go, when someone brings it up, we do not have to let it define us any longer. Instead we can say, "Thank you Jesus, I'm a new creation now," and move on. Let us continue our journey of discovering our new identity starting right now.

In order to move forward in the fullness of our new identity we must change our mindset. Renewing our mind with the Word of God daily is critical because it changes our old thought patterns and removes the old garments worn by the old person. Romans 12:2 says, *"And do not be conformed to this world, but be transformed by the renewing of your mind, that you may prove what is that good and acceptable and perfect will of God."* Recognizing that our life now is found in Jesus alone helps us move with purpose and not get stuck in the past. Let us continue learning about our new identity and put on our new attire. Old things have passed away and God is doing a new thing in us.

New Garments

Accepting Jesus as our Lord and Savior allowed us to receive a new identity and fabulous makeover. Makeovers are usually given to individuals wanting a change of appearance. They may cut or dye their hair; change their wardrobe and anything else that presents their best version of themselves.

Many spend countless hours adorning themselves on the outside and pay little attention to the condition of their heart. While meticulously fixing the outside and ensuring that everything is in place, we can be full of ugliness inside. The Lord told Samuel exactly how He views us, *"...for man looks at the outward appearance, but the LORD looks at the heart"* (1 Samuel 16:7). God is not impressed with how we look on the outside. Some people look at us and conclude who they think we are before ever getting a chance to know us. In fact, if they do not like how we look, some even shun us. What if God did us this way? No, instead He looks at our heart. Instead of aiming to dress to perfection, we need to check our heart. The best makeover we will ever receive is letting Jesus dress us and complete us from head to toe; transforming us inside out. He removes our stony heart and gives us a heart of flesh. Our attire is tailor-made when Jesus makes us over. Isaiah 61:10 says:

> *...He has clothed me with the garments of salvation, He has covered me with the robe of righteousness, as a bridegroom decks himself with ornaments, and as a bride adorns herself with her jewels.*

There are garments we may need to allow Jesus to remove. Certainly we won't put designer clothes on top of old dirty ones. In fact, not many people like wearing dirty clothes at all. This is not to imply that we must try to get things together before coming to God, because only He can change us.

Colossians 3:8-10 says:

> ...put off all these: anger, wrath, malice, blasphemy, filthy language out of your mouth. Do not lie to one another, since you have put off the old man with his deeds, and have put on the new man who is renewed in knowledge according to the image of Him who created him.

Why would we want to walk around wearing filthy rags when we have clean clothes available? Ephesians 4:22-24 also tells us about other useless garments we need to allow God to remove by renewing our mind with the Word of God. *"...put off, concerning your former conduct, the old man which grows corrupt according to the deceitful lusts, and be renewed in the spirit of your mind...put on the new man which was created according to God, in true righteousness and holiness."* Love is the most fashionable garment we will ever wear and it must first be received in order to be put on.

Nothing compares to the love of God. His love changes us. We do not have to try to hide our flaws, but instead when we come to Him concerning areas of our life that are in need of change, He is willing to take off the old garments and give us fresh ones as a great exchange.

Colossians 3:12-14 says:

> *Therefore, as the elect of God, holy and beloved, put on tender mercies, kindness, humility, meekness, long suffering; bearing with one another, and forgiving one another, if anyone has a complaint against another; even as Christ forgave you, so you also must do. But above all these things put on love, which is the bond of perfection.*

Just as we get regular health checkups from a physician, it is equally vital to do regular spiritual checkups. A spiritual checkup helps us grow spiritually and monitors the condition of our heart. Before most of us leave home, we look in the mirror to check our outfit and appearance, when instead we should check if we are wearing our best garment—God's love.

We Are Accepted and Secure

As God's children, He accepts and loves us the way we are. Rest assured, we do not have to pretend or try to impress Him because nothing we do shocks Him. Maybe if we made heaven and earth we could, but God did that already. Think about it, He even created us and when we feel inadequate remember, He does not call those who are qualified, but qualifies those He called.

Some people may treat us as less than a child of God or refuse to associate with us if we fail to meet their standards, but our Father will never reject us or abandon us when we fall short of His expectations. We are accepted and loved.

Too often we find ourselves seeking the approval of others but God already loves and accepts us as is. Knowing I was accepted and loved by God helped me through a lot of tuff times in my life and was live-changing. Though I experienced much pain and hardships, my anchor and foundation was the solid love of God. Despite the trials of life, we were always loved by God, and He had us in mind before the world began. Ephesians 1:3-6 says:

> *... just as He chose us in Him before the foundation of the world, that we should be holy and without blame before Him in love, having predestined us to adoption as sons by Jesus Christ to Himself...by which He made us accepted in the Beloved.*

I know firsthand about being adopted into a family. The first time I read Ephesians 1:3-6, it pierced my heart because the realization of God choosing to adopt and accept us into His family before the foundations of the world were established, resonated with me. It brought me back to a clear resemblance of my adoptive parents being chosen by God, before I was born, to be my first examples of His love. They treated my twin and me as their beloved own. The thought of being accepted and loved by parents who did not physically birth us, yet treated us as their own is heartfelt. They safeguarded us from this wicked world. Had they not adopted us, I'm not sure where I would have been, but I know my life would have been much different. The more I process just what they did for my brother and I, it shows me how much God loved us by giving us parents with hearts the size of Texas. They welcomed us into their hearts, home and family.

An adoptee is recognized as an heir and entitled to the family inheritance by way of inheritance rights. Similarly, God has adopted us into His family by way of Jesus and we are His sons and daughters. In Him we have an inheritance and receive a hundredfold all that was lost, (see Mark 10:29-30). He also provides refuge, and never abandons us or treat us like we do not belong in His family.

In Him, we do not have to fear being rejected or abandoned because we are accepted and loved, (see Isaiah 43:1-2). As members of the household of God, we can go boldly before the throne of grace to a loving Father who accepts us.

We Are Heirs of God

As heirs of the kingdom of God we have an inheritance. The possessions and treasures of God are far beyond anything we could ever imagine. We are royalty because we belong to the King of kings and Lord of lords. Romans 8: 16-17 says, *"we are children of God, and if children, then heirs—heirs of God and joint heirs with Christ..."* We are God's beloved children and no longer slaves. While we are not bound to our past, the enemy will always try to use it against us, because if he can get us tangled up, we cannot move forward in our God-given identity, (see Galatians 4:7; and Galatians 5:1). We are Heirs of God's promises on earth and in heaven. His Word is His Will. His Living Will shows us exactly what He left to us but if we do not read it, we will never know what belongs to us.

We Are Unique and Have Great Value

Each individual was uniquely created by God with purpose and has great value. If God created us; we are valuable! We are not junk, mistakes, rejects or throwaways. When the apostle Paul addressed the church at Corinth, he asked what we should be asking ourselves now, *"Do you not know that you are the temple of God and that the Spirit of God dwells in you?"* (1 Corinthians 3:16). God's Spirit is living inside of us, consequently His presence in us makes us of priceless value. We also have all we need to live successfully because we have Him living inside of us. A reminder of our value comes from Matthew 6:26 when Jesus said, *"Look at the birds of the air, for they neither sow nor reap nor gather into barns; yet your heavenly Father feeds them. Are you not of more value than they?"* Certainly, we are more valuable to God than birds. If He takes care of them, surely, He will take care of us. As we look to Him as Jehovah Jireh, our Provider, we do not need to become overwhelmed by circumstances that appear uncertain because God will take good care of His own. All the days of my life God has always been faith and took care of me. As the righteousness of God, we must also have a clear distinction from the rest of the world. 2 Corinthians 5:21 says, *"For He made Him who knew no sin to be sin for us, that we might become the righteousness of God in Him."* Our thoughts, speech, and actions also should display our identity, in terms of the character of God. Matthew 5:13 says, *"You are the salt of the earth; but if the salt loses its flavor, how shall it be seasoned? It is then good for nothing but to be thrown out and trampled underfoot by men."* Choosing to walk in the flesh causes us to lose our flavor. Those around us should see our light and know we are children of God. Others should sense something different about us. Ephesians 5:1-2 tells us, *"...be imitators of God as dear children. And walk in love, as Christ also has loved us..."* If we carry ourselves otherwise, we are viewed as hypocrites. Having a bad attitude and blending in with the world also dims our light. We cannot be both light and darkness. Nobody is perfect and we all make mistakes, but we should repent and turn away from sin. Our identity in Jesus is more than what is conveyed here and we must continue learning about who we are and our worth in Him. Knowledge of our identity in Jesus allows us to be all God purposed for us.

We Have Purpose

God created us for a specific purpose. Since we are ambassadors of Jesus, we represent the King of kings and Lord of lords. As God's living epistles—letters read by men; those around us should see Jesus working in our life. How are we presenting Jesus to others? Are we living purposeful lives? Do we act one way at church and another in different settings? To know what specific assignment God wants us to do, we must read the Word of God, and spend time inquiring of and worshipping Him. 2 Timothy 1:8-9 says:

> *...share with me in the sufferings for the gospel according to the power of God, who has saved us and called us with a holy calling, not according to our works, but according to His own purpose and grace which was given to us in Christ Jesus before time began.*

As ambassadors, we all called to the Great Commission, to take the gospel to the ends of the earth, (see Matthew 28:18-20). An ambassador of Christ is an authorized representative or messenger who represents all that He represents. It is important to know Him in order to represent Him. As representatives of God, we carry-out His work on earth, and have purpose, (see John 15:16).

Confidence in the Lord

Our confidence should be in Jesus alone. He promised to complete His work in us and work great and mighty exploits thru us as His Spirit works in us. God is not done working on us. Philippians 1:6 says, *"being confident of this very thing, that He who has begun a good work in you will complete it until the day of Jesus Christ."* Confidence should be found in knowing that continuous and honest communion with the Lord, allows Him to transform us from glory to glory. Confidently knowing and understanding that God will finish the work He started should encourage us to trust the process and plan that God is working in our life. He is faithful and will never give up on us. As we seek God with our whole heart, we can live confidently because our best is yet to come. God has promised us a marvelous future. When life appears uncertain, we can always find confidence in the Lord because He loves us and wants the best for our life.

Chapter 4

Self-love

TO LOVE OTHERS genuinely, we must first love ourselves. Self-love (philautia) is a healthy practice, that is instrumental in sacrificially loving others, and differs from philautos, discussed in chapter one. Self-love however becomes a problem when we are arrogant and prideful.

A common misconception about self-love is that loving yourself is a prideful act; and depending on the approach taken, this belief could be truthful. However, the kind of self-love expressed here is not philautos, narcissistic; selfish, arrogant, conceited or an attitude of being superior to others. Instead, this approach learns to fully accept and respect oneself as God's creation. Philautia is also thought of as friendship with one's self; and an act of respecting the person God created.

Opposite of loving ourselves is hating ourselves. If we dislike ourselves, then loving others will be nearly impossible. Truly loving others and ourselves can only be accomplished once we connect to God's love because God is the source of love. Additionally, loving and knowing our identity in Christ is essential for living an impactful and victorious Christian life. As a result, we take better care of ourselves and others.

Loving ourselves involves more than simply grooming our outer appearance. Fully loving ourselves involves focusing on the complete person—body; soul (mind, will, emotions and intellect), and spirit—allowing us to live our best life. To embrace growth, we must also realize God wants us to flourish and to live abundantly. 3 John 1:2 tells us, *"Beloved, I pray that you may prosper in all things and be in health, just as your soul prospers."* When we love ourselves, then we can be the best version of the person God created us to be.

Learn to Accept Yourself

Self-love involves learning to accept who we are; flaws and all. While there may be things we desire to change, learning to love who we are right now is important for growth. And as we pray for help to strengthen our weak areas and those needing change, God does things His way, and in His time, with love.

Accepting who we are not only requires loving every part of ourselves, but also forgiving ourselves from the past. Letting go of the past involves releasing regret, and disappointment, which allows us to move forward and focus on the new things God is doing in us. Once we accept ourselves, then we can allow God to work on areas needing improvement without beating ourselves up. No matter who you are, there is some area that can be improved.

Continuous Growth and Development

Self-love involves growth and improvement both inward and outward. God's love strengthens us to go through the process of growth and development. Assessing where we are personally is necessary to target specific areas for growth. Once our direction becomes clear, we can focus on identifying and eliminating any repetitive or contrary routines that deviate from our goals. A clear focus of what is to be accomplished will keep us on track to reach our goals.

Becoming aware of areas needing improvement is accomplished by taking a truthful assessment of where we stand. Acknowledging our strengths and weaknesses is a tool toward growth. Otherwise, we live deceived and do not reach our full potential. To correctly assess, we must ask God to reveal our status and He may convict us in some areas. Our assessment should always be measured by the Word of God—truth. Living Christ-centered lives involves confronting blinding beliefs that stagnate us from moving forward. No longer are we slaves to these repetitive mindsets that once ruled our body, mind and emotions but now we live according to the Spirit and our thoughts and actions should align. Romans 8:1-2 says:

> *There is therefore now no condemnation to those who are in Christ Jesus, who do not walk according to the flesh, but according to the Spirit. For the law of the Spirit of life in Christ Jesus has made me free from the law of sin and death.*

If we are led by the Spirit no longer do we yield to the dictates of our flesh. Instead, we have God's Spirit living inside of us and have self-control and freedom. There will always be weaknesses and areas in life needing improvement and we should always seek godly counsel.

As we explore specific areas in our life that shape our overall wellness, we can expect God to expose things that need improvement. Understand, the insight given here is not to go against your licensed professional within their respected fields, however God's wisdom is beyond man's comprehension. When God uncovers things to us, it is wise to pay attention.

Components of Wholeness

To have a healthy balance in areas that encompass wholeness there must be a willingness on our part to change and adjust as necessary. Familiar routines keep us stuck in our comfort zones and habits. Change is not always easy when we take a new approach or new steps in an unknown direction. In fact, most people never follow their dreams because of fear. No looking back now, because greater things are ahead. The areas of our focus will include physical wellness; emotional and mental wellness, intellectual wellness, social wellness, environmental wellness, occupational wellness, financial wellness and spiritual wellness. Each subject outlines a guide from a biblical stance; to help us identify where we are, and provides a plan to move in the right direction.

Physical Wellness

Loving one's self physically means taking care of the body internally, as well as externally. In doing so, we care for our bodies from a point of understanding it is the temple of God. Prosperity is connected to financial, spiritual and physical wealth and God wants us to prosper spiritually as well as physically, (see 3 John 1:2). All aspects of physical health are considered, as well as, utilized to the best of our ability from this understanding. For instance, we get proper rest; eat healthy, and exercise regularly. The healthiest food we could ever feed on is the living Word of God.

Loving our body causes us to take actions that promote healthy living. However, exercise alone is not the only essential tool for maintaining a healthy body. 1 Timothy 4:8 tells us, *"For bodily exercise profits a little, but godliness is profitable for all things..."* Above our priority for physical improvement, should be a willingness to make our lives available to God.

While grooming, personal hygiene, and caring for ones self is important, consecrating our body to God is of utmost importance, because we are to "...present your bodies a living sacrifice, holy, acceptable to God, which is your reasonable service" (Romans 12:1).

When a person takes care of his or her body as the temple of God, it is an act of self-love and obedience to God. Many insecure people attempt to project their insecurities on those exercising self-love and caring for themselves as the temple of God, however every child of God should love him or herself and realize his or her value. We should respect ourselves as God's creation; a royal and chosen people.

Emotional and Mental Wellness

A major component in emotional wellness is learning to handle changes in life. Having an awareness of our emotional state is critical to our health. We all have emotions and cope differently. Sometimes men and boys are told not to cry, but Jesus cried. No two people are the same and the way they deal with their emotions will vary from person to person.

One may experience many emotions throughout a day, however understanding even though the emotion is present, acting on it is optional. For instance, one can be angry and not react or give in to the emotion. Our emotions do not control us when we walk in the Spirit of God. Being saved does not mean our soul wounds have been healed. There may be areas we have not given to God. In fact, many who have emotional scars from their traumatic pasts are in this category. Only God can heal deep emotional pain, memories or scars from our past. Unaware that I needed emotional healing, I carried soul wounds for many years after giving my life to Jesus, before ever seeking soul healing. Allowing God to heal our soul removes pain we may be carrying and replaces it with the love of God.

A balanced life minimizes stress levels and foster emotional wellness. Life brings good and bad stressors, that can trigger our emotions. Granted, some situations and circumstances present stressors we never anticipated. There are however areas within our scope we can adjust to minimize stress. Identifying those areas are key to living and maintaining emotional and mental wellness. For instance, maybe someone decides to begin eating healthy. Throughout the day, he or she struggles to find healthy meals. A conscience adjustment to manage this emotional stress could be meal planning. Balancing also includes other disciplines, like learning when to say no.

Recognizing areas that cause emotional strains and making necessary adjustments, minimize stress overall. On the other hand, mismanaged stress usually leads to a negative outcome and hinders production and focus. It also effects other areas of life, such as the body, and may even lead to physical ailments.

Self-Love

Outside influences can also play a role in our emotional wellness. However, anything contrary to God's Word is a hinderance to our emotional wellness and spiritual growth. For instance, what we hear and watch; places we go, and the people we socialize with, all influence us either beneficially or detrimentally. Surrounding ourselves with nurturing support systems; healthy relationships and having a positive attitude are great ways to improve our emotional wellness.

Additionally, being mindful that situations and circumstances are never permanent, and trouble does not last always. Jesus is the only constant in life; everything else is subject to change, but He remains the same yesterday, today, and forever, (Hebrews 13:8). He has good plans for us. Our current situation is temporary and will eventually change, allowing us to experience new options, opportunities and life lessons. Despite the difficulties we may face in life, Philippians 4:8 says:

> *Finally, brethren, whatever things are true, whatever things are noble, whatever things are just, whatever things are pure, whatever things are lovely, whatever things are of good report, if there is any virtue and if there is anything praiseworthy— meditate on these things.*

Our emotions may leave us feeling as if no one cares or loves us at times, but that is a lie. Even when we feel unloved or forgotten, God never stopped loving us. Instead of focusing on the negative, there is always something to be thankful for and ways to enjoy life and be content with whatever state we find ourselves. For instance, finding healthy and enjoyable activities to participate in can relieve our stress.

Every person is different and has different ways of releasing tension. Therefore, you must find what works best for you. Some people journal; workout, pray, vacation, get massages or golf. Of course, nothing trumps being filled with the love of God and abiding in the peace of God. However, if your emotional or mental wellbeing is compromised and you need to speak to someone, do not feel ashamed to ask for help. Get professional help immediately and do not suffer silently.

Intellectual Wellness

As long as we are alive, there should be a desire to be lifelong learners. There is always more that we can learn no matter how old we get. If we are teachable, we can learn from those older or younger. Gaining knowledge helps us grow, however our intellect should never be placed above the wisdom of God. Wisdom starts with knowing and reverencing Jesus as Lord. Proverbs 1:7 states, *"The fear of the LORD is the beginning of knowledge, but fools despise wisdom and instruction."* God gives us wisdom and understanding liberally, if we ask. Not only should we desire wisdom, but also a thorough understanding.

Social Wellness

God did not create us to live isolated lives. Socializing is important and gives us an opportunity to put others before ourselves. Jesus interacted with people from all walks of life. Likewise, our interaction with others should be with all people and not only those who look similar or share our beliefs. Hebrews 10:24-25 tells us, *"...consider one another in order to stir up love and good works, not forsaking the assembling of ourselves together..."* Coming together is beneficial because we encourage one another and bear one another's burdens.

Socializing is important and in healthy relationships, boundaries are established. Positive social wellness includes; knowing our boundaries, as well as, those of others within our relationships. Since people are different, boundaries within each relationship will vary from person to person. We should never feel bad about setting healthy boundaries or disconnecting from toxic relationships that subject us to abuse. Maintaining a healthy social life is being mindful of our contact and connections with people we allow into our life. Healthy social wellness also encompasses knowing when to let go of destructive relationships that create havoc in our life, as well as discerning when to allow healthy ones to enter.

Environmental Wellness

Our environment plays a huge role in our overall wellness. The quality and condition of places we go either add value or take away from our life because environments affect our health.

Interestingly, studies found an astonishing correlation between room color and changes to one's mood. For instance, the color yellow in the kitchen was found to speed up one's metabolism. Our senses (smell, touch, sight, etc.) detect energy in different environments. What we take in thru our body affects us. Ever go somewhere and sense the energy in the atmosphere? Was the place welcoming or hostile?

Our home is the place we generally spend the majority of our time and should be clean, clutter-free and peaceful. Ever enter someone's home and immediately feel the warmth? Being mindful of our surroundings also promote healthy environmental wellness. Creating a positive atmosphere in the environments we frequent is conducive for our environmental wellness.

There are some ways we can promote healthy environmental wellness. For instance, the presence of the Lord should be invited everywhere we go, because His presence is freedom and peace. Another way to promote environmental wellness is being aware of changes we can make to foster a peaceful environment. How can we change the climate in the environments we frequent? First, we need to ask some important questions: What environments do I frequent? Are these places beneficial or detrimental to my life? Are there adjustments that can be made to improve my environment? Avoiding some places altogether demonstrates the love and respect we have for ourselves.

Occupational Wellness

When people have a career or job they enjoy, it brings a sense of fulfillment and happiness to their life. Even those who do not get paid for jobs they love still find joy in doing something they love. While listening to the radio one day, a woman called into the radio station as she drove to a new job. She explained it was her second day of doing a job she absolutely loved; and her previous job was dreadful. The excitement she had going to her new job was obvious. If possible, working in a field you enjoy, promotes occupational wellness.

Too often people are stuck doing jobs that merely pay the bills. They are unhappy and feel inadequate because they want to be doing something else. Understandable, it is not always feasible to quit a job instantly and jump into a new career, however if we take steps toward our goal each day, eventually we can get to where we want to be in life.

Fear can keep us paralyzed from moving toward our goals. We need to ask some thought-provoking questions: Are we currently doing what we enjoy? If not, what obstacles are in the way? What strategies can help us realize our goals? Remember, everyone has to start somewhere, so never despise small beginnings. Analyze, adjust, and execute while understanding, nothing is impossible for God.

Financial Wellness

Financial freedom allows us to experience life in ways we would not be able to otherwise. When one lives in poverty or lack, it affects his or her overall wellbeing. In this condition, the individual is living below their full potential. God wants us to live abundantly in every aspect of our life; including our finances.

Poor financial manage and choices lead to financial ruin. A healthy relationship with money promotes better financial choices and freedom. Financial freedom allows us to do things we enjoy without worrying about our finances. The best thing we can do with our finances is give tithes and offerings, because when we give God what already belongs to Him with gladness, He blesses our finances. There are numerous promises concerning the prosperity of those who love and honor God. Malachi 3:10 tells us:

> *Bring all the tithes into the storehouse, that there may be food in My house, and try Me now in this, says the LORD of hosts, if I will not open for you the windows of heaven and pour out for you such blessing that there will not be room enough to receive it.*

Our finances are impacted by our giving or lack thereof. Whenever I failed to tithe, my finances were always negatively affected and I would have lack. On the flip side, ever since I began tithing and giving offerings, there has not been any lack in my life and God always provides for me.

There are steps we can take to improve our finances. First off, if we fail to give tithes and offerings to God we need to start right there because we bring a curse to our finances when we fail to do so, (see Malachi 3:8-9). Once that is in order, then we can begin to get our finances together and make changes that move us in the right direction. Having a budget and sticking to it is one way to manage our finances. Given, there may be unforeseen circumstances and adjustments will be necessary, however, budgeting helps to manage finances.

The following questions are important to ask: Do I have more money coming in, than expenses? If not, how can I earn more income or cut expenses? How am I spending my money? Are there areas where my expenses can be lowered? Do I need help managing my finances? A person that is unable to develop a financial plan may need assistance. In such case, it may be wise to take a money management class or hire a licensed professional to on the journey towards financial wellness.

Spiritual Wellness

Growing spiritually requires a continual effort to seek God and spend time with Him daily. If we love God, spending time in the Word daily and mediating on it day and night, will be our response. Given, there may be instances when this is no possible. Additionally, carefully examining ourselves and applying the Word to our life is necessary for spiritual growth. As we seek the face of God—His Word—He draws near to us and we grow up in the spiritual things of God.

In the love of God, we are constantly being taking from glory to glory and that is why it is important to abide in His love (covered in chapter five).

Regular spiritual assessments are necessary if we want to continue developing and living the abundant life that God has called us to live. An honest assessment is vital in each area of wholeness we covered if we desire growth and development in body; soul (mind, will, emotions, and intellect), and spirit. Some questions to ask ourselves include: What areas do we need growth? What changes can we make to reach our goals? In what areas do we need help to reach our goals? What are we doing well that needs to be maintained? Pray and ask God to direct our path, growth, and development and to be led by His Spirit.

Chapter 5

Abide in Me

GOD TELLS US to abide in His love. Abiding in the love of God is ongoing—endless despite situations or circumstances; and is an expression of our love, trust, and obedience towards God. *Abiding* is defined as a feeling or memory lasting a long time; and enduring or continuing for a long time.[8] Romans 12:9 tells us, *"Let love be without hypocrisy. Abhor what is evil. Cling to what is good."* By holding on to the goodness of God, our life should reflect the love of God, as we abide in His love. We must remain in a position of love towards God and others and not be moved by any means.

Remaining in His love adds blessings to our life and allows us to embrace the joy of the Lord, which is our strength. It also produces character, strength, hope, patience, love, peace, and perseverance. In the love of God, we have all that we need because it gives us access to everything connected to God. Therefore, abiding in the love of God gives us the fullness of

God. John 15:9-11 Jesus says:

> *As the Father loved Me, I also have loved you; abide in My love. If you keep My commandments, you will abide in My love, just as I have kept My Father's commandments and abide in His love. These things I have spoken to you, that My joy may remain in you, and that your joy may be full.*

In Him alone do we have everything needed, because *"...all things work together for good to those who love God, to those who are called according to His purpose"* (Romans 8:28). Many times, I sought things outside of God, but only when I made Him first in my life did I find peace and everything I needed, (see Matthew 6:33).

Remaining in His perfect love also cast out fear, because anything not of God cannot remain in His presence. As we abide in Him, we are able to face our fears, knowing that He loves us and is in control of all things. Fear may try to stop us from doing what God has called us to do, but He has not given us a fearful spirit. We are bold and courageous. When we bring our fears to God we can trust Him to handle any circumstance or obstacle presented to us.

Trusting God

Trusting God can be challenging during troubling times or in times of uncertainty. Life can even present horrific circumstances that make it hard to get out of bed and face a new day. When we do not put our trust in God alone, the challenges of life can be overwhelming. Remember, His mercies are new each morning and trouble will not last always.

An understanding that God alone is in control of everything and His ways are above ours, should put our mind to ease. We may become frustrated by things that are out of our control or meant for only God to know. Some events in life make no sense. Trying to analysis or figure them out, often leads to frustration. At other times, we may feel alone and wonder, *"Does anyone see me? Does anyone hear me?"* It may have even appeared at times that nobody cared or understood, but I want you to know, God never leaves or forsakes us. He sees, hears, and knows all things. Most importantly, He can be confidently trusted in times when everything appears shaky. God is faithful!

Trust issues can form when we have been hurt, and especially when it comes from those closest to us. After a person has been betrayed repeatedly by those he or she trusted, they began to put up walls or defense mechanisms to prevent being hurt again. Ever tell someone your innermost secrets in confidence thinking it would be concealed, yet and the next day it was broadcasted on a microphone? Then we build walls or learn to use wisdom and caution when sharing information with others, however, we can trust that God will protect us.

God is not like man because He can be trusted completely with everything. Faith in God's promises allow us to know He can be trusted even during difficult and uncertain times. During some of the most difficult times in my life, I found solace knowing that God could be trusted no matter what was happening in my life. Faith in God's promises also sustained me, because I knew His Word as truth. In His Word I found my Help and Strength as I meditated on the Holy Scriptures to get me thru. There were days I doubted and wanted to crawl under a rock, but every time I cried out to God, He assured me I could trust Him. Sometimes things changed immediately and at other times things remained for a lengthy period. One thing I know for sure; God is faithful and He will never let us down. All my life God has been faithful. Deuteronomy 7:9 says, *"Therefore know that the LORD your God, He is God, the faithful God who keeps covenant and mercy for a thousand generations with those who love Him and keep His commandment."* God knows those who trust Him, and He shows Himself trustworthy and faithful, (see Nahum 1:7).

People may disappoint or let us down, but God is always faithful and keeps His promises. Remember, we are never alone. God promised never to leave us nor forsake us and will be with us always. His Spirit lives inside us. 1 John 4:13 say, *"...we know that we abide in Him, and He in us, because He has given us of His Spirit."*

Trusting God involves giving Him our whole heart. Giving Him our life means we give Him access to all areas of our life. Proverbs 3:5 says, *"Trust the Lord with all your heart, and lean not on your own understanding; in all your ways acknowledge Him, and He shall direct your paths."* Trusting God involves having our mind settled on serving Him for the rest of our life. God is faithful and we should be as well. Our obedience to God causes Him to reveal even more of Himself to us. John 14:21 says, *"He who has My commandments and keeps them, it is he who loves Me. And he who loves Me will be loved by My Father, and I will love him and manifest Myself to him."* God desires for us to get closer to Him and let go of anything causing separation. He promises to show more of Himself to us when we obey His Word.

What Can Separate Us?

God's love cannot be taken away from us. It is our choice to either get closer to Him or put distance between ourselves and God. Sure our relationship will be tested by different pressures of life, but nothing is able to separate us from God unless we allow it. Absolutely nothing stops God from loving us or desiring a relationship with us.

We have victory to overcome every trial that comes our way when we are connected to God. Romans 8:35-39 asks:

> *Who shall separate us from the love of Christ? Shall tribulation, or distress, or persecution, or famine, or nakedness, or peril, or sword? ...Yet in all these things we are more than conquerors through Him who loved us. For I am persuaded that neither death nor life, nor angels nor principalities nor powers, nor things present nor things to come, nor height nor depth, nor any other created thing, shall be able to separate us from the love of God which is in Christ Jesus our Lord.*

This is a thought-provoking question that demands a reply. Absolutely nothing can separate us from God's love. If our relationship with God gets better or worse, understand; we decided to either put distance between God and ourselves or to get closer. We should never let anything interrupt our relationship with our Savior. Are there things in our life we have allowed to interfere with our relationship with God? Whatever we place before God becomes our god or idol.

God's proper place should always be before anything or anyone. For all the love He has shown us; devotion to Him should never be burdensome. Instead, our response should be faithfulness towards the One who is faithful to us.

At some of the most difficult times in my life, God was the only One there for me. And even when people try to help, some voids only God can fill. I cannot help but give Him praise and my life because it belongs to Him alone. Throughout life, I have always been able to trust God and He never failed. When death knocked at my door several different times, He protected and saved me. God was my constant when everything else was finicky.

God remains the same yesterday, today and forever, (Hebrews 13:8). He is constantly calling us to deeper fellowship. Things change for the best when we have a mind settled that nothing will separate us from God.

IN THE NEXT SECTION, WE DISCUSS LOVING AND SERVING OTHERS.

PART 3:

Loving & Serving Others

Chapter 6

Unity

UNITY AND LOVE go together. All Humanity desires love in some capacity, whether we admit it or not. In many ways, there is a desire to be united with others. Unfortunately, imperfect people carry their flaws and relational issues—jealousy, ageism, pride, control, gossip, racism, hatred, etc., —where they go, and unity is not always realized.

Even the thought of being rejected and unloved cause emotional trauma for some. Others hide behind masks, pretending not to need anyone, and then seek extreme measures to fill their longing. Beneath the disguises, we simply desire love.

A desire for love is displayed in many relationship structures: husband to wife; parent to child; peer to peer; and so forth. Our interaction with others also ranges from complicated companionships, to peaceful partnerships; and comprise of those we love or hate; have forgave or need to forgive; respect or disrespect, and so forth. We will look at some relationship structures to understand unity and love in our relationships.

For love, many have done things they may or may not be proud to admit. Most can agree, at some point they pursued love in a toxic manner. In a Miss Dior commercial, a woman asked an interesting question, "And you, what would you do for love?"[10] As innocent as this question appears, responses would be shocking as they reveal the absurd things people do for love. For instance, some will choose to be with someone that is incarcerated for life. On a lighter note, others seek things that are not necessarily bad, but provide false gratification to fill their longing for love.

There are many counterfeits that try to duplicate the love of God, but at best, they only give temporary satisfaction. Seeking wholeness in relationships outside of our personal relationship with Jesus will always leave us disappointed. Even people with "good intentions" let us down at times. They cannot provide what only God can, because they are flawed as well.

Receiving love from others is pale in comparison to the love of Jesus and typically has some sort of condition, restriction or limitation. Additionally, people say they love us, yet their actions may prove otherwise, and undermine or inflict great pain. If we fail to meet their expectations in word or deed, some even turn their back to us. However, God is the faithful One, always there to comfort us, as only He can. One unaware of this truth seeks love and fulfillment in all the wrong places.

Nothing compares to God's love. Although we give and receive love from others, only God's love completes us.

Jesus does not love us the way we love. His love is perfect, because He is perfect in all His ways; including His love for us. Nothing nor anyone can be what God is to us. Think about it; He is love. How could anyone provide greater love than the Source of love? To be fully content, one must have a personal relationship with God, otherwise he or she will have a void. Understand, to be in unity and love with others, we must abide in the love of God. True, God did not create us to be alone, however a clear understanding that nothing compares or is greater than His love allows us to prioritize the importance of our relationship with God.

The love of God serves as our model for loving others. Receiving His love is necessary before we truly love others. We must first receive the love of God personally, and continue to abide in His love, to genuinely and unconditionally love others. Why? Because we cannot give what we do not have. As our relationship with God improves, our relationship with others improve as well. He gives us strength to love, forgive, and have healthy relationships with others, when we allow Him to fill us with His love.

Covenant Relationships

Our relationship with others should replicate the perfect love Jesus has for the church. He loves us unconditionally, despite our shortcomings, and showed this by laying down His life to rescue us from sin and death, while we were sinners. He remains faithful and loyal even when we are unfaithful to Him. The love God has for us is the kind our covenant relationships should follow, because it demonstrates the highest form of love we can offer others.

A covenant relationship was seen between Jonathan and David. They shared a special bond, and *"...the soul of Jonathan was knit to the soul of David, and Jonathan loved him as his own soul"* (1 Samuel 18:1). Jonathan could let his guard down and be vulnerable before David. He trusted Him with his robe, armor, sword, bow and belt. Jonathan giving his robe to David symbolized a covering. Likewise, we should cover one another in love and prayer. 1 Peter 4:8 says, *"And above all things have fervent love for one another, for 'love will cover a multitude of sins."* Jonathan's loyalty towards David caused him to risk his relationship with his own father because he honored the covenant they made with each other. Our covenant relationships should be valued and appreciated. Unfortunately, not many can be trusted or loyal, as David and Jonathan.

Love based on a condition being met, is not agape love, and definitely does not resemble God's love. Loving God's way goes beyond loving those who are kind to us or those who share our similarities. Unconditional love also involves loving our enemies; those who we know hate us, betray us, and mistreat us. Ouch! Loving and sacrificially serving others puts their needs before our own. We should love and cherish those in our lives today, because they may not always be there.

Loving the agape way is not always easy and certainly challenges us at times, but with the love of God abiding inside us, unconditionally loving others is possible.

Loving Others as Ourselves

We are called to put others before ourselves. Exercising the golden rule to treat others, as we want to be treated is a good example of loving others as ourselves. By serving and respecting others, even when they mistreat us, we demonstrate agape love. Galatians 5:13 tells us, *"...through love serve one another. For all the law is fulfilled in one word, even in this: 'You shall love your neighbor as yourself.'"* We must "be examples of love" toward others and love the way Jesus loves the church. Ephesians 4:1-6 says:

> *...walk worthy of the calling with which you were called, with all lowliness and gentleness, with longsuffering, bearing one another in love, endeavoring to keep the unity of the Spirit in the bond of peace. There is one body and one Spirit, just as you were called in one hope of your calling; one Lord, one faith, one baptism; one God and Father of all, who is above all, and through all, and in you all.*

The church is a connected body. One single body. Since we are members of one another, to love others is literally to love ourselves. Esteeming others above ourselves, demonstrate our love for others as ourselves.

Remembering that we have not always been where we are right now should help us treat others with agape love, compassion, and mercy. We never should look down on others, but uplift and encourage our fellow brother or sister; being kind and creating peace with everyone at all costs; including those who do us wrong. Matthew 5:9 says, *"Blessed are the peacemakers, for they shall be called sons of God."* While it can be difficult at times to love this way, God honors peacemakers, and we must love people where they are. Meaning at times we have to love people in their hatred; pain, struggle, jealousy, and frustration.

Not all relationships result in special bonds or covenant relationships, but we can welcome peace towards all people. We must love our enemies. Tolerating abusive or bad behavior certainly is not what is being implied. Instead, we should understand the influence we have on those we reach.

Our interactions with others should always be peaceful and loving on our part, no matter what. The way we treat others impact; either good or bad. There may however be times when we have to set boundaries for people who mistreat us. Keep in mind, it is not always evident what a person has gone through or may currently be experiencing that is triggering their behavior. The way we treat people always matters. This is true even when we are mistreated. The way we choose to use our influence impacts others. Jesus did not model ugly behavior and neither should we.

We are the hands and feet of Jesus on earth and should represent Him well. Loving everyone as if they were our own family members is how we love others as ourselves. Proverbs 18:24 tells us, *"A man who has friends must himself be friendly, but there is a friend who sticks closer than a brother."* Jesus loves us like no one can and put us before Himself by sacrificing His life so we could be saved. Some of our closest relationships come outside of those related to us. Marriage is a covenant relationship that God uses to display His love for the church—His bride. Jesus is coming back for His bride and we will be with Him forever.

Marriage

Marriage is a covenant relationship highly esteemed by God. However, no relationship including marriage provides love and security like God's love. The church is the bride of Christ and represents a type and shadow of the marriage and wedding taking place at the return of Christ. Before marriage, we need to be made whole in the love of God and continue abiding in His love afterwards. Many people get married believing somehow, they will be happier once married, only to realize that only God is capable of providing us love and joy.

Trust me, based on personal experience, marrying the wrong person has consequences. Only when both are equally yoked and transformed by God's love can they genuinely love each other the agape way; as Christ loves the church. If a person has not accepted God's love and then gets married, he or she joins their brokenness with their spouse and is worse off than being single. Be patient and trust God to bring the one He prepared for you before the foundations of the world to avoid misery.

Singleness

A single should focus on oneness and unity with God. Singlehood is not necessarily a bad or permanent statue. Nor does it mean something is wrong with the individual or that God loves him or her any less. Wanting to be married is not wrong in and of itself, because God created us to be in union with others. Singles can however live full lives by accepting and embracing the love of God and all the benefits of living a single life in unity with God. Marriage requires more responsibilities and less personal time to fellowship with God.

Society often places negative stigmas and demands on singles. However, those that know who they are in Jesus do not accept negative labels that others try to place on them. Content singles let the love of God fill them and use their season of singleness to prepare for a spouse, if that is what he or she desires. Again, this shows how we should be preparing ourselves for the return of Christ, and His bride. Singles, wait on God to send the spouse He predestined just for you, in the meantime, pray and use the time wisely to allow God to fill you with His love. Then when your spouse comes, you will be prepared and enhance him or her instead of subtract from his or her life.

Be still and complete in God's love before joining with anyone. Understand that our Maker is our first Husband (Isaiah 54:5) and loves us like none other. News flash, a person who is unhappy being single, will be unhappy married because happiness comes from within. Deal with the root of why there are feelings of discontentment. If you are considering marrying someone but unsure, a good indicator that you should not marry him or her is if he or she does not bring you closer to God. It should not matter how much money he or she has; how he or she looks or what type of car he or she drives. If the relationship causes conflict between you and God, choose God. Being with someone for the sake of having them is dysfunctional.

When we allow God to fill us with His love, we can live a content life whether we have someone or not. After all, no person can love us more than God, because He is love.

Unity Theme

When people are united and walking in love towards one another, it pleases God. Unity and peace should be our theme song. As one Body, we need each other because our relationships with each other is important for us to do what pleases God. Since we are one Body, there must be unity with all members and not just those we have been grouped together for a long time.

As the connected Body, our interactions should be more than simply gathering. We should genuinely love one another; and carry the burdens of others. When one hurts, we all hurt. Likewise, when one gains, we all gain. We must carefully discern the hour we now live in, knowing we need each other now more than ever. While writing this book, the church is being persecuted all around the world. Will we be grouped among those persecuting or with those supporting the Body?
As our focus becomes clearer, and our goal set before closer, we see anything attempting to distract or sideline us from the things of God much clearer. Strife and discord is a tactic of the enemy to get us to fall out with each other and divide, and not focus on doing the work of the Lord. On the other hand, our unity and bonds bring us together to do His work.

Unity and love allow the blessings of God to flow. When we are walking in discord, strife, and in our flesh, God is not happy. However, it pleases Him when the Body is operating in unity, peace and love. Psalms 133:1-2 say:

> *Behold, how good and how pleasant it is for brethren to dwell together in unity! It is like the precious oil upon the head, running down on the beard, the beard of Aaron, running down on the edge of his garments.*

In Ephesians 4:11-16 Paul says:

> *...gave some to be apostles, some prophets, some evangelists, and some pastors and teachers, for the equipping of the saints for the work of ministry, for the edifying of the body in Christ, till we all come to the unity of the faith and of the knowledge of the Son of God, to a perfect man, to the measure of the stature of the fullness of Christ; ...speaking the truth in love, may grow up in all things into Him who is the head—Christ—from whom the whole body, joined and knit together by what every joint supplies, according to the effective working by which every part does its share, causes growth of the body for the edifying of itself in love.*

Each member of the Body is needed and no member is more important than the other.

We all have gifts and talents given by God to be used to build the Body. When we fully grasp that we are on the same team and of the same Body, no longer will we see each other as competition or envy others for doing what God appointed to them. No longer will be slander and belittle those who come alongside and partner with us. Instead we will comprehend the bigger goal ahead, and our vital roles as a part in the Kingdom of God; each one working together with a new perspective to accomplish what God assigned to us individually and collectively as a corporate Body. Assimilating any other way make us decapitated and not intact as the Body. Picture an arm in one location, a leg and hand yet somewhere else. In that situation, the Body is severely disabled; lacking components that help it grow and function properly. Imagine if only fingers associated with other fingers and never met the mouth, the whole body would starve.

The Body of Jesus functions as a unit. What if a new addition to the Body was rejected? Liken that to a mother rejecting her newborn baby, but praying for an extended family. As the Body grows, are we welcoming and nurturing? Do we want our family to remain as usual? After all the prayers for lost souls, do we treat others like they do not belong or as if we are superior? Do we welcome them to the table thinking they are dressed inappropriately and have not washed their hands? Not one person in this world is perfect or better than the next. Jesus said, *"Let him who is without sin cast the first stone*, (see John 8:7)." We all are in need of a Savior. God looks at our heart and not our outward appearance. We should never look down on people because of our differences. Condoning inappropriate attire is not what is being conveyed here, however, if someone did dress inappropriately, who are we to judge them? Ever think that may be all they own? Some also judge others based on their past or rumors they hear before ever getting to know people. Sadly, some people even judge people based on how they worship.

While we should not worry about what people think of us, we must realize judging and mistreating others bring division. Further, we have been warned about what causes division and divisive language and coarse jetting is included among factions and gossiping.

2 Timothy 3:2-5 says:

> *...men will be lovers of themselves, lovers of money, boasters, proud, blasphemers, disobedient to parents, unthankful, unholy, unloving, unforgiving, slanderers, without self-control, brutal, despisers of good, traitors, headstrong, haughty, lovers of pleasure rather than lovers of God, having a form of godliness but denying its power. And from such people turn away!*

All these behaviors lead to division. It is easy to embrace what we find familiar. Often unaware, people gravitate to those they can relate or share commonalities. On the other hand, separation created by others is intentional. In heaven there will not be a "black church," "white church," "Hispanic church" or any other distinctive church dividing the Body of Christ. Why are such things happening on earth? Maybe the division is unintentional or out of fear. Are we are lacking the love of God, which our precious faith is built on, and which casts out fear? Whatever the case; we must fully understand what is written in Ephesians 2:19:

> *Now, therefore, you are no longer strangers and foreigners, but fellow citizens with the saints and members of the household of God, having been built on the foundation of the apostles and prophets, Jesus Christ Himself being the chief cornerstone, in whom the whole building, being fitted together, grows into a holy temple in the Lord, in whom you also are being built together for a dwelling place of God in the Spirit.*

As the "fullness of Christ," we must have our hearts knit together in love. Everything about Jesus reveals coming together collectively as His Body, and doing His work thru us, for His glory. As the Body of Christ, we are all one. Ephesians 2:14-16:

> *For He Himself is our peace, who has made both one, and has broken down the middle wall of separation, having abolished in His flesh the enmity, that is, the law of commandments contained in ordinances, so as to create in Himself one new man from the two, thus making peace, and that He might reconcile them both to God in one body through the cross, thereby putting to death the enmity. And He came and preached peace to you who were afar off and to those who were near. For through Him we both have access by one Spirit to the Father.*

As the body of Christ, we should move forward to close the gap between division and unity.

Living in unity and peace is a choice. Identifying areas in our life that cause division and deciding to make necessary adjustments towards unity is a start. To assist in accomplishing this, the next chapter is geared on helping us identify areas of improvement and how we can live in unity and peace with others.

Chapter 7

Challenging Relationships

LOVING OTHERS CAN be difficult sometimes. People are complex and each individual has unique characteristics and qualities that distinguish him or her from another. No two people are the same, and everyone has a different personality. People do not always get along.

Imagine if love was shown year-round and not just during peaceful holidays, such as Valentine's Day; Easter; Thanksgiving and Christmas. Can you visualize how different the world be? With God's Spirit Living inside us, all that is needed to love people three hundred sixty-five days a year, is within and readily available. 2 Timothy 1:7 says, *"For God has not given us a spirit of fear, but of power and of love and of a sound mind."* God's Spirit dwells within us and we can love always.

To identify some issues causing division, we look at specific issues that cause conflict in relationships. We also learn how to handle them from a biblical prospective. As we look at relational conflicts, the Word of God serves as our manual for handling challenges faced in relationships. First, we must understand why we have conflict.

2 Timothy 3:2-5 says:

> *...men will be lovers of themselves, lovers of money, boasters, proud, blasphemers, disobedient to parents, unthankful, unholy, unloving, unforgiving, slanderers, without self-control, brutal, despisers of good, traitors, headstrong, haughty, lovers of pleasure rather than lovers of God, having a form of godliness but denying its power. And from such people turn away!*

One way to minimize relational issues is by examining ourselves to ensure we are not practicing any of the characteristics mentioned in 2 Timothy 3:2-5.

God tells us to love everyone, including those we find difficult to love. When we are filled with the love of God, and a challenge to love "difficult" people or those we find "hard to love," presents itself, God expands our capacity to love regardless of the circumstances.

If we are not walking in love, we are walking in strife. Proverbs 10:12 says, *"Hatred stirs up strife, but love covers all sins."* Where there is strife, know that all manner of evil is there as well. 1 Corinthians 3:3 asks, *"...For where there is envy, strife, and divisions among you, are you not carnal and behaving like mere men?"* As children of God we need to be in unity, not strife. Likewise, we are not to follow false doctrine, teaching or get into useless debating among ourselves. If these situations occur, we are told how to handle such matters.

2 Timothy 2:23-24 says, we should *"...avoid foolish and ignorant disputes, knowing that they generate strife. And the servant of the Lord must not quarrel but be gentle to all..."* Some things are not worth entertaining, especially foolishness.

Despite our attempts to love and maintain peace with some people, they may still reject us for no apparent reason. In which case, we have to love those people from a distance. People do not always accept one another, but we must be kind and respectful to everyone at all times. Romans 12:18 tells us, *"If it is possible, as much as depends on you, live peaceably with all men."* God blesses peacemakers (see Matthew 5:9).

It is easy to snapback at people that mistreat and disrespect us, especially for no apparent reason; however, there is a better way. In Matthew 5:44 Jesus says, *"But I say to you, love your enemies, bless those who curse you, do good to those who hate you, and pray for those who spitefully use you and persecute you."* We must love and pray for our enemies even when they mistreat or persecute us unjustly. Understand, when we pray to God about situations and get out the way, He intervenes on our behalf. *"...for the battle is not yours, but God's"* (see 2 Chronicles 20:15). Do you love and pray for your enemies? If not, then began to and watch God intervene.

Since people are flawed and broken, there will be times we experience relationship issues, however, walking in God's love and forgiveness allows us to love everyone.

Bad Company

Toxic and unhealthy relationships drain the life from us. These associations leave us feeling worse off and wishing we never linked up with that particular individual at all. Growing up, momma would tell me not to keep "bad company." In other words, do not have covenant relationships with troublemakers or bad influences. Eventually, if we hang around a person long enough, we pick up some of their habits; the good or bad ones.

The Bible tells us not to keep company with corruption and those who practice evil. Proverbs 1:15-16 says, *"My son, do not walk in the way with them, keep your foot from their path; for their feet run to evil, and they make haste to shed blood."* Not everyone is moving toward God, and we have to be wise to not be sucked into a trap of the enemy, by making covenant relationships with them. Further, everyone should not have full access to our life if they are not moving towards God; however, you must still love them. We have to be careful not to get pulled away from God by associating with bad company.

The quality of our relationships are far greater than the length of time we associate with or know one another. For instance, a thirty-year friendship between two individuals who don't trust one another, lacks quality. How can we truly have covenant relationships with those we do not trust or know secretly envy us? Unfortunately, only after we spend quality time with some people do we realize they are troublemakers all along and refuse to change.

Relationships go thru changes. When we ask God to reveal the quality of our relationships, He will and some people are in our lives for a short period and others a lifetime. Some challenge us to do better and others want to destroy us. Some have an assignment or purpose to fulfill in our life before they are gone. We must learn to value those in our life today.

Misunderstandings

Misunderstandings are inevitable, but the way we handle them makes all the difference. At some point, things we do and say will be interpreted incorrectly. In Joshua 22:9-34, a misunderstanding occurred at Shiloh in the land of Canaan between the tribe of Reuben; Gad, half the tribe of Manasseh and the children of Israel. The group had good intentions and a common goal to serve the Lord, but a misunderstanding caused the children of Israel to gather against each other.

When Phinehas and the other leaders confronted Gad and Reuben about accusations made against them, they discovered all was not as it appeared. They were unclear why the altar was built, but this discrepancy could have caused a devastating outcome, had it not been settled. Phinehas, priest of the rulers and son of Eleazar, perceived the truth after hearing the matter out. The situation could have gone a different route and ended badly, behind a simple misunderstanding, had they not come face-to-face. Interacting face-to-face and quality time spent with others is important to develop meaningful relationships.

With social media platforms on the rise, the "new normal" way of communicating comes by way of posting or thru text message. The problem with this method of communication is messages can easily be taken out of context and also ruin wholesome friendships. Additionally, subliminal messages are posted on social media sites towards people, in hope that they see them, instead of picking up a phone or having a conversation with them. However, they are often unseen and the offended person remains just that. Subliminal messages leave people left to perceive intent based on tone and delivery; and gives room for things to be misunderstood or causes division. Although we may not always understand the actions of people, it is wise to receive clarity before jumping to a conclusion, as it promotes unity and love.

Gossip

Words are powerful and can be used in positive and negative ways. Wholesome friendships and covenant relationships are ruined by gossips. A person that cannot hold a word spoken in confidentiality usually cannot be trusted otherwise. Ever have someone that you trusted in confidentiality spread your secret to others? Sharing details about another person without their permission is gossip. Sometimes we share things about another without an intent to harm the individual, but the person we told tells another and rumors spread.

Nobody wants to befriend a person who talks about others and spreads rumors. Some people will dislike others and spread lies about them, in effort to get others to dislike them also, which causes division. Talking about another person without praying for them or offering assistance puts us in position to gossip. Some people use praying for another as an excuse to gossip and talk about others business.

Not everyone is capable of holding information discussed in private. Using wisdom before revealing information to others is essential to keeping unity. Gossips want to be the first to run and tell information and spread rumors and lies about others. Proverbs 16:28 tells us, "a perverse man sows strife, and a whisperer separates the best of friends." Being mindful of our conversations will prevent gossip.

Thinking before we speak helps us to not just say whatever comes to mind or engage in gossip. When we have a problem with another person, we should go directly to them and try to straighten things out instead of talking about them with others.

When people bring gossip to us, we can decide not to partake in the conversation. If a person brings something to our attention concerning another person, instead of gossiping, we should pray for that individual or situation. Otherwise, we are also part of the problem. We must also use wisdom to know what should only be between God and ourselves. Psalm 141:3 says, *"set a guard, O LORD, over my mouth; keep watch over the door of my lips."* Use wisdom in speech because our words are powerful and can cause division.

Insecurities

In some form or fashion, we all deal with insecurities. Learning to love the person God created us to be helps build our confidence. Understand, nobody but God is perfect, and we all have flaws, insecurities, and weaknesses. Insecurities are seen thru jealousy; approval addiction, envy, coarse jetting, judging, betrayal, belittling, intimidation, competition, comparison; among other things. Many insecure people try to project their insecurities on others because they are unhappy within and attempt to break the spirit of others by insulting or belittling them. As we know all too well, misery loves company. We should never let others project or place their insecurities on us.

Approval from others never should define us. If we let the opinions of others validate us, then we are taking our eyes off God and allowing people to qualify or disqualify; value or disregard, and label us. Expecting others to validate us only leads to disappointment because, it is impossible to make everybody happy all the time. We must stop expecting others to pat us on the back or applaud us because only God can approve or disapprove us. Just because people have opinions about us, (trust me, they will have opinions), does not make their opinions factual or even valid.

Pleasing and obeying God alone should be our focus. If He justified and approved us, and says, *"job well done,"* that is the only approval we need. When we know that He accepts and loves us, we freely live to be all that He called us to, without fear of anyone.

Pride

Pride effects the quality of our relationships. Where pride is present, we will see many people competing with each other. The Word tells us, *"By pride comes nothing but strife, but with the well-advised is wisdom"* (Proverbs 13:10). A prideful person makes everything about self and interacts with others selfishly. Prideful people desire to be the center of everyone's attention all the time and fail to esteem others before their own interests. They try to make others appear inferior by constantly putting them down or get mad when they do not do things their way. A prideful person's agenda is exalted above others and does whatever it takes to make things go their way. We cannot discuss pride without addressing ego because everyone has a sense of self-esteem or self-importance. However, a prideful person constantly needs their ego stroked or pampered.

Confidence is not to be confused with pride. Confidence, however becomes a problem when a person places their trust in anything other than God. Pride places deep assurance in one's ability for achievement, instead of total reliance on God. Pride is puffed up. Proverbs 16:18-19 tells us, *"Pride goes before destruction, and a haughty spirit before a fall. Better to be of a humble spirit with the lowly, than to divide the spoil with the proud."* A prideful person will be humbled by God because as God's children, we are called to live humble lives.

Jealousy

Jealousy is deeply rooted in insecurity. When people do not have enough confidence in who God created them to be or understand they have something unique to offer others, they focus on others and make comparison. Jealousy also causes division because we cannot have covenant relationships with those who secretly envy or compete with us. Some people are jealous for no apparent reason, and others have particular reasons they become jealous of others.

Immediately after my parents passed, I moved from California to New Jersey with an older brother. The move brought new surroundings; a new school, new friends, and new enemies. One day while in gym class, a group of girls decided to team up against me for being "the new girl." As we stood waiting in line to be dismissed from class, someone pulled my ponytail. Everyone looked clueless when I turned around to see the culprit. Thinking somehow it was a mistake, I turned around facing the front of the line. The next pull whipped my neck backwards, and clarified any suspicion of an accident. Again, I turned around to see who pulled my hair, but no one owned it, so I faced forward again. However, when my hair was pulled aggressively for a third time, I quickly turned facing the group with all the frustration pinned-up from losing my parents and said, "Whoever is pulling my hair, bet you won't do it while I'm looking." I was ready to lay the whole group down, no lie. Apparently, it showed on my face, because the gang of bullies looked shocked as I looked each in the eye. Later, it was brought to my attention the girl pulling my hair was jealous of me because her boyfriend took an interest in me. The funny thing was, I had no idea and meanwhile thought she was the coolest one at the entire school, (of course until she pulled my hair). After all, she was beautiful; wore the latest fashions, everyone liked her, and she was smart. While I admired her, she secretly disliked me and was jealous about things out of my control.

The moral of the story: comparing ourselves to others causes us to lose sight of the grace and beauty God has given each one of us. We all have something that only we can offer. Our gifts; talents, personality, laughter, and love is invaluable and uniquely ours. Each person has something special to offer others and therefore, we need others to be the best version of who God created them to be.

Hatred

Hatred is the opposite of love and those operating in this manner are walking in the flesh. The Bible also tells us, those practicing such will not inherit the kingdom of God, (see Galatians 5:19-21). Some people hate others without cause. It may not have been anything they did to warrant the hatred. Others may hate people for specific reasons, such as, their beliefs; race, economic or political background.

Unfortunately, many people have been senselessly killed behind the face of hatred. Although there may be people who hate without cause, we must still choose to love them regardless. When we are hated by others we need to get a clear understanding that they are being used by the enemy. In doing so, this allows us to handle hatred with love, and prevents us from slapping the fire out of someone. Especially when they provoke us. Ephesians 6:12 Tells us:

> *For we do not wrestle against flesh and blood but against principalities, against powers, against the rulers of darkness of this age, against spiritual hosts of wickedness in the heavenly places*

No matter how hard we may try to close the gap between unity and hatred, some people will allow the devil to use them, as they choose not to love; respect, or value some people. Regardless, we still are supposed to love everyone always.

1 John 4:8-11 says:

> *He who does not love does not know God, for God is love. In this the love of God was manifested toward us, that God has sent His only begotten Son into the world, that we might live through Him. In this is love, not that we loved God, but that He loved us and sent His Son to be the propitiation for our sins. Beloved, if God so loved us, we also ought to love one another.*

When we experience hatred, our dealings are with an evil spirit operating thru that individual. There will be times when people hate us. Keep in mind, Jesus was perfect in all His ways, but was literally hated to death without cause. Certainly we are not greater than He and our response should always be that of love.

Chapter 8

Forgiveness

IN A WORLD full of different cultures, religions and opinions; disagreement and conflict is sure to arise from time to time when interacting with people. As we connect with others, there may be times when an offense comes out of nowhere. One important thing to understand is that we can choose to live in unforgiveness and be offended or we can choose to forgive and let it go.

Surprisingly, unforgiveness and offense have been linked to cause known health issues and are classified as a disease. Research by Dr. Michael Barry, found a sixty-one percent relation of all patients harboring unforgiveness, that were linked to cancer.[11] Unforgiveness has negative consequences. Further, unforgiveness and offense directly affect us and prevent blessings from flowing to our life. Without a doubt, there may come a time when we get offended. Understand, when we choose to not forgive others, it puts us in bondage and directly affects our quality of life. The word *forgiveness* in Hebrew is *aphiemi, charizomai* or *aphesis* meaning, to send forth; send away; to remit or forgive; to bestow a favor unconditionally; a dismissal or release.[12]

Knowing how to handle offenses or situations where there is tension is critical. When we are offended, love is not flowing freely and our faith is built on love. If love is not operating in us, our faith in not working properly either, because love is the greatest gift of all. Therefore our *"...faith [is] working through love"* (see Galatians 5:6). We can trust God to deal with those who mishandle us and most importantly, choose to walk in love. In Luke 17:1-4, Jesus spoke to the disciples saying:

> *It is impossible that no offenses should come, but woe to him through whom they do come! It would be better for him if a millstone were hung around his neck, and he were thrown into the sea, than that he should offend one of these little ones. Take heed to ourselves. If your brother sins against you, rebuke him; and if he repents, forgive him. And if he sins against you seven times in a day, and seven times in a day returns to you, saying, 'I repent,' you shall forgive him.*

Jesus exaggerated the number of times that one must forgive others in a day, because He knew we would face offensive situations and may need to forgive many times.

Choosing not forgive others holds us hostage to the situation and is a snare from the devil. The word *offense* in Hebrew is *skandalon* meaning, a trap to which the bait is attached; or stumbling block.[13] Offense is bait and a stumbling block that opens the door for the enemy to access our life. Understanding this should make us want to stop and think of everyone we need to forgive and choose to not be offended by others. Are there people we may need to forgive? In other words, are there people the devil used to trap us by way of offense, that we need to let go? As Christians, we must handle conflict correctly.

When Conflict Arises

A clear understanding of forgiveness as a choice allows us to rise above conflict. In choosing to forgive, those who caused the offense are released from our heart, and we exchange the offense with the love of God. As Christ forgave us, we forgive them.

  One of the hardest things I had to do was forgive those closest to me that caused my greatest pain. I thought to myself, God will punish them because He knows what they did to me. Although God knew exactly what was done, it did not excuse the fact that I needed to forgive those individuals for hurting me. For seven years, I carried unforgiveness in my heart. The moment I decided to forgive, I literally felt the weight lift off my body, and was lighter. I realized for nearly a decade, I was causing myself harm by choosing not to forgive and holding on. The entire time I was deceived and thought I was hurting them, when in all actuality, they carried on with their life unbothered. Unfortunately, we sometimes wait around for an apology we will never get from those who wronged us. They go on with life, but we continue hurting and harming ourselves by what they did or did not do to us.

When I chose to forgive all the people I held hostage in my heart, I was freed in that moment and realized the power of forgiveness. After all those years, I was the one suffering instead of those who harmed me. The painful things I went thru gave me a prospective on the power of forgiveness altogether. From my experience, I pray others will also gleam the freedom and power associated with forgiveness.

Although forgiving others is not always easy, it truly is more for us, than for those who cause us pain, because when we forgive others, God forgives us. If God forgave our sins we committed against Him, and chose to die for us, we should also choose to forgive others.

Handling Offense

There will come a time when we are offended by others and when others are offended by us. There may also be times we offend people by doing absolutely nothing to them (from our prospective). For instance, our very presence can be offensive to some people. In situations when we know others have an unjust issue toward us, we are supposed to go to them in love and try to work it out.

Confronting someone who has an offense toward us without cause can be more challenging than forgiving someone who clearly did us wrong. For instance, addressing someone known to have an issue with us without cause, may leave us feeling uncomfortable or as though the problem belongs to him or her, especially when unsure of the issue to begin. The more we try to ignore a situation, usually the problem worsen. Most times, we wish the conflict would somehow disappear. We may think ignoring the problem altogether will cause it to vanish. However, dismissing issues usually get out of hand until they are addressed. Once we have tried to resolve things with that individual or individuals, if they decide to harbor offense, then that is between them and God. In Matthew 5:22-24 Jesus tells us:

> *...whoever is angry with his brother without cause shall be in danger of the judgment...Therefore if you bring your gift to the altar, and there remember that your brother has something against you, leave your gift there before the altar, and go your way. First be reconciled to your brother, and then come and offer your gift.*

Our goal toward unity and peace will allow us to humble ourselves and go to our brother or sister in love to mend things. In this same manner, when we are offended, we must choose to forgive others who have wronged us. Colossians 3:13 says, *"...if anyone has a complaint against another; even as Christ forgave you, so you also must do."* God is not concerned with our gifts or talents when we are walking in offense toward others and there are problems between His children. He hates discord and strife.

At all costs, we need to walk in love with everyone. Note, when we go to our brother or sister to fix an issue, we must go to them in love and respect, not rage. Addressing those who have an issue with us, allows unity to flow between those involved. Since God loves unity and calls His people to live in harmony, keeping unity among the Body of Christ should be our focus. Who are those in our life that we have an issue with or know has an issue with us? We must humble ourselves and choose unity.

Unity is not being practiced when offense is present. As we explained, holding on to offense and grudges has major consequences. Harboring offense and unforgiveness causes bitterness and anger. Forgiving others is more for us, then for the person that caused us pain. If we do not forgive others, God will not forgive us. Is anyone worth forfeiting our opportunity to be forgiveness by God? When we choose to not forgive others, we do just that. Additionally, choosing not to forgive hinders God from freely moving in areas of our life. Let's see how unforgiveness hinders our prayers. Jesus says in Mark 11:23-26:

> *... I say to you, whoever says to this mountain, 'Be moved and be cast into the sea,' and does not doubt in his heart, but believes that those things he says will be done, he will have whatever he says. Therefore I say to you, whatever things you ask when you pray, believe that you receive them, and you will have them. And whenever you stand praying, if you have anything against anyone forgive him, that your Father in heaven may also forgive you your trespasses. But if you do not forgive, neither will Your Father in heaven forgive your trespasses.*

Disagreement hinders our prayers. Our prayers are hindered, not those we have unforgiveness toward. When we hold on to strife or hatred, it pollutes our heart and traps us.

Holding offense blocks love from flowing and our faith does not work without love, because the greatest of all is love. Our *"...faith [is] working through love"* (Galatians 5:6). God is not concerned about our gifts when unity is at stake. Too often, when we are mistreated, our belief is that the burden falls on the other person to apologize or ask for our forgiveness. However, when we know they hold an offense towards us, we must try to straighten things out, Though they probably should ask us for an apology. Many times, we may never get the apology we believe we deserve.

There may be situations where we tried to mend an offense, however the friction remains. In such case, Jesus tells us in Matthew 18:15-20:

> *...if your brother sins against you, go and tell him his fault between you and him alone. If he hears you, you have gained your brother. But if he will not hear, take with you one or two more, that by the mouth of two or three witnesses every word may be established...whatever you bind on earth will be bound in heaven, and whatever you loose on earth will be loosed in heaven...if two of you agree on earth concerning anything that they ask, it will be done for them by My Father in heaven. For where two or three are gathered together in My name, I am there in the midst of them.*

Maintaining unity is important. When we walk in agreement with others, God in the middle of it all and our prayers are powerful. On the flip side, if the enemy can keep us walking in strife and discord with each other, we forfeit unity and agreement.

Reconciliation

There are situations that cause people to fall out and separate from one another. Sometimes these relationships can be restored, however that may not always be the case. Although we can choose to love people where they are, despite their weakness, it may not always result in a restored relationship. If a relationship is not able to be reconciled, we must continue loving that individual, even if it has to be done from a distance.

Often overlooked, is our ministry of reconciliation, which calls us to be one in the Body and fully understand His plan to reconcile all to Himself. Likewise, as the Body, we should be reconciled to those who are separated from us. Division is not on God's agenda and it should not be on ours. All His sons and daughters have been redeemed thru Jesus Christ. 2 Corinthians 5:18-20 says:

> *Now all things are of God, who has reconciled us to Himself through Jesus Christ, and has given us the ministry of reconciliation, that is, that God was in Christ reconciling the world to Himself, not imputing their trespasses to them, and has committed to us the word of reconciliation. Now then...be reconciled to God.*

We see that God did not hold us to our trespasses we committed against Him, but forgave us. We also must forgive and be reconciled, and not divided. In Jesus, we are His body; displaying His love on earth. Nothing compares to the love of God. His love never fails!

~Appendix~

Lord, Come Into my Heart

RECEIVING JESUS INTO your heart is the best decision you will ever make. "...if you confess with your mouth, the Lord Jesus and believe in your heart that God raised Him from the dead, you will be saved (Romans 10:9)." Salvation is a free gift. Jesus said, *"Behold, I stand at the door and knock. If anyone hears My voice and opens the door, I will come in to him and dine with him, and he with Me* (Revelations 3:20)." The prayer below invites Jesus into your heart. To accept Jesus as your Savior now, **Repeat the following prayer**:

Dear Lord Jesus, I recognize that I am a sinner in need of the Savior. I confess and repent of all my sins and ask You to forgive me and cleanse me of all unrighteousness. I believe You died on the cross and rose from the grave. Come into my heart and live there forever. I make You Lord and Savior of my life. In Jesus' name. Amen

Welcome to the family!

You are now a child of God; saved, forgiven, and redeemed. Now, do not stop here. Take these steps to continue growing spiritually:

- Pray that God shows, leads, and teaches you in all His ways. Read the Bible daily, to get closer to God, and abide in His love.

- Find a local church of like-minded believers.

- Get baptized.

- Continue believing and trusting God on this life-long journey.

"...as many as received Him, to them He gave the right to become children of God, to those who believe in His name"
John 1:12.

Do you want additional books?

You are welcome to visit www.bcrosspublishing.com or www.bettymcross.bigcartel.com for additional books and resources. This book is also available at major retailers by request.

Have a testimonial or want to share your progress? Visit our website today or join our newsletter to receive updates and information about events and new releases.

May God richly bless and fill you with the love of God. If this book was a blessing to you, please share your experience with someone.

Endnotes

1. *Merriam Webster's Collegiate Dictionary,* 11th edition (Springfield, MA: Merriam-Webster, Inc. 2003), 688.
2. *W. E. Vine, Vine's Concise Dictionary of the Bible (Nashville, Tennessee: Thomas Nelson, Inc. 2005, 225-226).*
3. *Ibid., 226.*
4. *Ibid., 2.*
5. *Ibid., 1.*
6. *Ibid., 226-227.*
7. *Ibid., 238-239.*
8. *Ibid., 162.*
9. *Ibid., 2.*
10. Dior: Miss Dior "For Love" Commercial. *iSpot.tv* 18 Jan. 2017. <https://www.ispot.tv/ad/Iktc/miss-dior-love-featuring-natalie-portman-song-by-sia>
11. *Johnson, Lorie. "The Deadly Consequences of Unforgiveness" CBN News. 22 Jun. 2015. WEB. 18 Jan. 2019.* <http://www1.cbn.com/cbnnews/healthscience/2015/June/The-Deadly-Consequences-of-Unforgiveness>
12. *Ibid., 144-145.*
13. *Ibid., 259.*

About the Author

BETTY M. CROSS is a California native but currently lives in Houston, Texas. She is a prolific writer and lyricist and her love for words lead to the production of many literary works. She has studied linguistics, Biblical studies, and child development for many years and holds a degree in liberal arts. Betty began teaching children at a young age and has also taught ESL students. Currently she is active in her community and works with the youth. Determined to pursue her dreams, she decided to trust God to use all He placed within.

www.ingramcontent.com/pod-product-compliance
Lightning Source LLC
Chambersburg PA
CBHW032127090426
42743CB00007B/502